love

lust

longing

&

Truth

love

lust

longing

&

Truth

by Jennifer L. Kite-Powell

cover and inside artwork by Chantal Calato

ISBN-13: 9780692961575
ISBN-10: 0692961577

author note

These works are an expression of my life as I wandered through Europe over the past eight years. They're tied to the cadence of my heart as I experienced love, lust, longing, and truth. I'd like to thank Chantal Calato who took the time to visualize the book in a way that echoes that cadence. I also want to thank Michael Taylor who was my sturdy muse and always insisted this book would happen one day. To Arican Wegter who told me never to erase the things that made me who I am. Tina Baker, who insisted I should do this one day as we sat on a sandy beach in Mexico; to Charlotte Krog who I conspired with over many cups of espresso and glasses of wine in our journeys together in Europe; and, to my cousin Shannon who knows my soul like no other. I hope you enjoy these poems.

artist note

The line, the most fundamental element of design, is explored in the art to reflect the heartbeat and mood of Jenny's poems. I am honored to have contributed to this book that clearly comes from the deepest and truest place of its creator.

table of contents

love

correlation

tides of stone
breezes of iron
molecules of lead

the air is heavy
the rain is light

a thought will suffocate
an idea will stagnate

hate fuels
fear ignites
the truth is not casual.

but love,
love does all those things

and, love does none of those things.

love is undefined, off the map, untamed, unbridled chaos
that fuels
ignites
suffocates
stagnates

and bends every molecule, neuron, breathe
and all the truth there is
into the thing that makes us human.

nostalgic whiplash

full throttle feels so good.
heart throbs, pulse careens.

flushing and blushing, heaving bosom Anna Karenina-style.

Tolstoy knew how to make a bosom heave in 200 words or less.

he had experienced the sweet spot that makes a woman flush and blush.

it's like starting my old 1976 Oldsmobile Cutlass Salon.
put the key in, turn it at just the right time
and then open her up.

full throttle feels so good.

then some asshole applies the brake,
and you forgot to buckle up.

ask someone to run really fast into a brick wall.
they won't do it.

love makes you do that.

karma

she's cursed
she's worshiped
she's distrusted

she's hated, loved and reduced to a cliche.

she's a saucy little minx
she's Pollyanna
she's a dictator and a flippant bitch.

she rides trains, hikes through the hills
and swims through the seas.

she gets lost in the wind
she drowns in a river
she stands alone.

she unfurled her lissome arms
and brought you to me.

pied à terre

he used to come over on Tuesdays to our little *pied à terre*
in the 11th arrondissement.

he'd text from Rue Lacharrière.

I'd start to tremble.

he'd buzz the building door at 18 Rue du Général Guilhem.

I'd start to shake.

there were three floors of Fibonacci stairs he'd have to traverse
to reach me.

I'd be out of oxygen by the time he got here.

I could smell him as he reached the last wooden step.

I could see my heart float out of my chest towards the door,
suspended in mid-air, looking back over its left pulmonary artery.

I reached for it, but it sputtered away closer to him.
It didn't even look back.

I was motionless.
it hovered.

the door started to shake as his hand touched the knob.

I reached out to stop it, but my heart fluttered to him.

he caught it in his perfect white teeth
and swallowed it whole.

bleating blob

I can hear my heart beating now,
but I never heard it before.

I can hear the blood surge
and race through my veins
straight to that beating blob.

a river flooding.
a stream spilling into its timid banks.
a bitorrent, only bloodier.

I hear my heart because I stopped breaking my own heart.

they never broke it
you never broke it
no one broke it but me.

my heart is mine to break, not yours.

now, the only heart I hear is mine.

do

don't tell me I'm sexy.
don't tell me I'm beautiful.
don't tell me you wish you had more time.

Is that all you have?

if you're brave enough, stop talking.

stop saying you'll take me in your arms.
stop saying you'll make me yours.

forget about the party.
it won't matter anyway.

it will be the same as it always was
unless you face what's inside of you.

you have me and you don't even know it.

blind raise

A declaration *d'amour* floats free in the breeze,
but no one sees it, no one grabs it.

one glass of champagne.
eyes fatally crashing across the gilded room.

that *declaration d'amour* is trapped in a bubble,
in a place no one dares to enter.

it's a garden of love filled with pleasure and pain.

the bubble makes me want to give you everything.
my utter nonsense, my imagination, my humility and my humanity.

I exist to be consumed by you.
I wait for you to swallow me whole.

but love is a Dead Man's hand.

there's no living in that bubble
and I can't break free of the invisible chains
that bind me to my fears.

C8H11NO2 + C10H12N2O + C43H66N12O12S2

ingredients: Dopamine. Serotonin. Oxytocin.

preheat the oven to a temperature that makes it
completely unbearable to function in your daily life.

mix all ingredients together in an iron-clad bowl lined
with epoxy and dipped in adamantium.

whisk for two minutes or three to six months,
don't use an electric mixer or add water, logic, sensibility or restraint.

heat to a low boil of schizophrenia, insanity and paranoia.

drain the extra froth.

serve immediately, garnish with a sprig of mint.

pair with Dungeness crab cakes and a glass of
rose on a pebbled beach overlooking the Pacific Ocean.

don't reheat.

original soundtrack

to feel the pain of you, brings desire.
the dark knight in you, brings light.
there's really nothing to see here,
except the door to another you.

I sit motionless in the middle of the world,
feeling the movement of everyone and everything.

except you.
you're lost.
being found is the problem,
not the answer.

indecent exposure

I can see you.

chemical imbalance

they all lied to me.
you're beautiful
you're smart
you're sexy
you're funny
you're a multi-faceted unicorn.

I'm none of these things.

I'm lazy
I'm fat
I'm spoiled
I'm weak

no one loves me, really.
they say they love me.
some feel biologically obliged to love me.

they don't.

no one has a clue what love is.
but, we do know what lust is because it feels so good.

but love?
it fucking hurts
stings
burns

crucifies
inhibits
rages
blinds
and sabotages who you really are.

love is the lie, why do they keep selling it?

ode to Harold Pinter

I bought your book of poetry
after listening to Julian Sands
bellow out your poems
and intimate moments
for one hour and 15 minutes
on a big empty stage
in Boise, Idaho.

one stage
one stool
one glass of water
and Julian Sands
in a dark blue suit
white collared shirt and
black wing tips
in Boise, Idaho.

I think he made you more real than reality made you.

I think he grafted all your pain,
brilliance
love
disdain
insistence
and,
frustration
to my psyche.

I think he made the words you strung together in a line
float out into that auditorium and land in the soft, spongy part
of my brain.

I think he made me love you
more than I already loved you.

in Boise Idaho, of all places.

lust

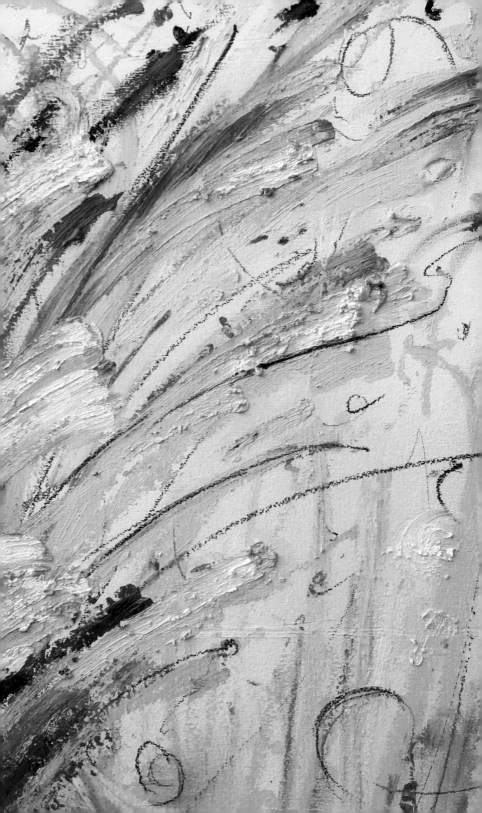

plant hedonism

confederate jasmine is just designer ivy.

like a highly manicured and over-styled stiff southern belle at
the country club, it only clings to the finest things.

its dark green waxy leaves,
as stiff as his morning erection,
form the scaffolding for delicate, white virginal blossoms
that fill the air with a hedonistic damp sweetness.

its invisible scent delicately floats around me filling the
pathways to my brain with an elixir of romantic narcissism.

that scent climbs all over me, laps at my ears
and slithers down my spine.

my body arches to meet its bewitching, sultry scent.

in a second it's over.

that should be an app.

heat

heat makes a paper cup sweat.

she's always slinking around by dignified old trees
sporting gray hipster beards made of Spanish moss which host a hive of
dog-day cicadas that took up residence in its branches.

they constantly broadcast their repetitive tune,
sucking in the heat and shoving it back at you
in a crescendo trance-like symphony.

heat pulls you under.

she's cruel.
she's a drug.
she seduces you to stand still when you don't want to.

you can't hide from heat in Chatham County, Georgia
It will find you.

escape into the arctic blast of Piggly Wiggly and it waits for you to exit.

her cicada emissaries taunting you with their
sultry heat waltz as you exit the store with hamburger meat
and cheap white wine.

the wine bottle even sweats.

if you walk barefoot under those beguiling bearded trees
their silvery beards droop and entice you to admire them.

it's a trap, she gets you again.

heat is a lover that never leaves.
she's a crime you can't escape.
a lie that won't release you.

ode to the guy in seat 21B

lovely little lashes embracing your icy blue optics.

New York City and Salt Lake City are forever burned in the
limbic system of my brain where memory is made,
turns to fantasy,

but never reality.

you said you wanted to drive with me really fast from Salt Lake
City to Boise, Idaho even though we might get a ticket
in Jerome County.

wherever that is.

The man in 22A was violating our moment by dry heaving his
Jerome County speeding story into our love nest.
something to do with speeding on the way
to the wedding of his wife's brother.

who cares.

you slaughtered him for me with one lash of your tongue about
the minivan he might have been driving.

my white knight.

you told me I seemed like a woman who was made for the autobahn.

whatever that means.

you were saying something about having a short connection.

but all I heard was let me take you off this 767 into the dead calm
of the salt flats outside of Salt Lake City, Utah in a 1972 black Dodge Charger
and love you forever.

private eyelashes

I saw him at the Pixies concert in LA.
I knew it was him from his lovely little lashes, Mr. seat 21B.

he was in the orchestra section three rows from the stage
smiling at Frank Black.

his head bobbed gently to Debaser.

I think he turned and looked back towards me.
I thought he looked happy.

was he looking for me all the way from Salt Lake City
at a Pixies concert in LA?

he returned to Frank Black and bobbed his head a little more.

I'm sure it was him.

Charles

two week stays in an over-priced,
cell block inspired Manhattan hotel
yield Charles.

that over-serving
shark catching
grinning bartender
knows how to mix a drink.

he leans into the bar.
carefully drinks your features.
sips your gaze.
fondles your words.

then it begins.

the glass
the booze
the condiments
the essence of something.

a glass slides to you.
his smile slides to you.

you drink the smile first
and taste the drink later.

them

tall. short. dark. light.

rough. smooth. sad. happy.

narcissistic. troubled. complicated. broken.

loving. drinking. fucking. laughing.

shallow.
vain.
shy.
robbed.

bourbon. wine. champagne. gin.

lies.

truth.

something in between nothing.

letters

I have 26 at my disposal
free of charge.
I can use them anyway I want,
no one can stop me.

I can abuse them with abandon,
indulge them with folly.

I can make them hopeless romantics.
I can turn them into hate.
I can create hope.
I can manifest fear.

I can orchestrate delusion, lust, avarice, sloth and pride.

I have so much power with just 26 symbols descended from
the lyrical cuneiform script that evolved from our guttural
grunts in a desperate attempt to proclaim existence and
mortality and express the prose of the various voices of our
infinitesimal lives.

26 at my beckon and call,

A B C D E F G H I J K L M N O P Q R S T U V W X Y Z

to make whatever I want.

touch

fill me up with a touch.

one shoulder.
one hip.
one gentle brush by my back.

let your hand linger.
feel my dress.
touch me.
just don't move your hand.

we don't remember what that feels like.

people don't touch anymore.

the internet has ravaged our sense of touch.

it's taken it from us and run off down
a dark alley of binary code.

I want to touch, to be touched, to smell touch.

just touch.

longing

seat 7A

airplane seat pockets are vile receptacles for traveler cast offs.

an unlikely hiding place for a furiously scribbled confession
from the passenger in 7A trapped there before you.

lost dreams, a Jay-Z concert,
a carnal tryst in a bourbon-scented
Westin Paris Vendôme hotel room
illuminated by half lit cigarettes
dying in a crystal ashtray.

just take a hit off her word syringe of love and discontent
and you know it ain't the lies that hurt,
it's the truth.

shut up

I can't stand the sound of your emails.

martinis, sweet tea & iced seawater

the spanish moss sways in the hot breeze over the dirty fringed
tiki-style umbrellas at Tubby's Tank House in Savannah, Georgia.

the waitress has eyes that are too far apart,
but in a good way.

she's got a face from a Flemish painting.
she doesn't know it.

her face doesn't fit her station in life.

she's 19.
she drinks vodka martinis with Grey Goose.
her boyfriend drinks Bud.

she speaks slower than she should for a girl her age.
her dulcet tones exaggerated by her desire not to work
or her desire not to hurry.

either way, she does little of each.

she wants to see the world.
she wants to drink Grey Goose martinis in Manhattan.

she won't.

she'll serve sweet tea and iced seawater in amber acrylic pint glasses dulled by 1,000 heavy-duty washes alongside primary-colored plastic baskets of fried shrimp in Chatham County Georgia day after day while those big, fat lumbering Savannah clouds, parked like mobster cars at a funeral where the land meets the sea, will dump that sweet Southern rain all over her big martini dreams.

Delta flight 45

I can't find you, you have no name, you have no number,
except seat 21B.

if our plane had crashed we would know each others names by now
and maybe we could find each other in the afterlife
wandering around asking if we were on Delta flight 45.

but, I don't even know where to start to find you.
there's no trace of you.

no footprint of you in a world full of footprints.

your digital signature is a flat line.

no line leads me to you, and a line should lead me to you.

a line always leads somewhere.

it starts in one place and ends at another unless you bend it
and then it becomes a circle and repeats itself over and over to infinity,
never ending like the snake eating its tail.

I am the snake eating its tail.

thor's *trompe l'oeil*

flip it, jump it, crash it.

219 months old is the sweet spot.
it's the apex of hope.
the g-sport of glory.
a chasm of infinity.

he's in between life and living.

living isn't caustic.
life isn't weighted.
fucking is just a thing you do.

emojis are his *trompe l'oeil*.

a flame to that one, two flames to another,
a heart for good measure.

no one really knows, the receiver interprets.

flip it, jump it, crash it
could just as easily be,
love me, know me, see me.

lost & found

where the sentence ends, the white space begins.

it's the Park Place of mental real estate,
the space where anything can happen.

it's the ecstasy of possibility.
and the agony of complacency.

it's there for the taking, but few take it.

it offers nothing,
but demands everything.

your l o v e
your p a i n
your j o y
your s o r r o w

it wants it all.

because it takes it all to fill the white space.

Google Hangouts in the upper east side

Google Hangouts is his telegraph pole.

it's his morse code,
his hail,
his shot across the bow.

smoke signal.
carrier pigeon.
dial up on a 1984 modem.

he wants to connect,
he needs to connect.

but he's stuck in the upper east side.

with her.

he knows what he wants,
he's afraid to take it.

every two months he puts up his telegraph pole
and hopes for a connection.

Mr. so and so

he never had me.
he only kissed me, Dr. Zhivago style.
but he kissed with intent.

intent is the betrayal.

intent to steal away into the night.
intent to devour me.
intent to behead anyone who got in the way.
intent to see giants in windmills, Don Quixote style.
intent to stand at the edge.

intent was his lie.

I hope intent kills him a little.

western world problems of the lowest degree

rain is an excuse to be lazy,
a justification for sloth.

the golden ticket to that other self
who lurks in that dimly lit,
poorly gardened
corner of your mind.

slanted, silvery, slivers of sloth.

slanted is the best.
cold is best.
Sunday is the best.

slanted, silvery, slivers of sloth on Sunday.

intravenous drip

I inserted the intravenous drip on a Saturday.

I used a delicate little butterfly needle
so I wouldn't feel the pain.

I wanted to feel something else.

I wanted to feel him inside of me as he flowed from the plastic sac
filled with gelatinous liquid that hung over my head on a skinny metal pole.

I wanted to feel him flood my veins with magnificent suffering
through a winding, sterile plastic tube.

an intoxicated drowning.
an exhilarating asphyxiation.

that needle fell out one day.
I think it was a Wednesday.

the thing is,
I'm not the same person I used to be after that feeding.

little parts of me peeled right off.

I could see them as they hit the floor around me
with that delicate butterfly needle still in my vein.

pieces of courage.
slices of esteem.
wafers of pride.
slabs of vulnerability.

choices I never saw.

pieces of me gone forever
through a delicate, sterile butterfly needle,
on a Wednesday.

tug of war

war in my heart.
death to my power.
murder in my soul.

the grains of discontent grow
as you subdue my light.

suffocate my being through silence.
end my breathe through withdrawal.

unbound by what once was bound,
which were the words that bind.

choking on the discontent
of my own expectations
which led me here,

to war with you.

because you put me in a glass box
where you can't hear my screams.

polyamorous existence

sometimes I can't see the point of anything anymore.

some guy is beating the shit out of his girlfriend next door
and I'm hitting rock bottom because my Tinder matches
all look the same.

ninety-nine percent of them say they're polyamorous
or they adore their kids, love to stay fit, dig beer and the outdoors.

oh, and no drama please.

I want to see a profile where the guy says his kids bug
the crap out of him and he just wants to cuddle after ordering a pizza.

or maybe he likes eating popsicles he bought
from the ice cream truck passing through his neighborhood
that he chased down in stealth mode wearing his 'I heart feminist' cap
on a beautiful summer day.

I'd love to meet that guy.

nothing tastes or feels the same anymore.
not even sex.

I drank a Tab the other day and it was off.
I'm sure of it.

did they ruin saccharin too?

summers are still hot,
but I'm not in swimming in a lake, water skiing
or drinking Miller Genuine Draft ponies.

winters are still cold,
but my coat isn't pink anymore
and definitely has no white, fluffy fur collar.

autumn is perfectly crisp, but rolling in the leaves
means you could also roll in shit.

spring is just stupid.

global warming has messed up that season,
so it isn't even the same.

I bet spring feels like I feel.

Truth

it's not what it looks like

palazzo
Italy
3 a.m.
table
letter
hangers still swaying in the antique armoire.

glass
wine
tears
punch in the stomach followed by a punch in the stomach.

husband
boxes
train
plane
gone

that switched me on.

you haven't lived until you get switched on.

futility

New York is a state of mind.

it's depraved.
it's angry.

full of discontent, malcontent,
contentious meat sacks filled with
lascivious, salacious intentions
in their hearts.

there's no soul in new york.
it's empty.
they only survive there.

they want your mind.
like a zombie wants your brain.

feel them coming?

they want you to care about the F train.
they need you to hate what they hate and love what they love.
they require you to become like them.

vapid
dissatisfied
Sisyphus clones drenched in futility.

everyone lies to you about New York.
they can't help it, it's the only way to survive.
to tell yourself white lies.
to create another reality on top of this one.

New York is the ultimate analog augmented reality.

they lie about the possibilities
because they know there aren't any.

they tell lies about being anything you want to be.

who wants to be anything?

how about being something?

epiphany by the river

people are ruined.

sucker punch

it's another life.
the one you dream of and get down on your knees for.

but, you can't have it.

instead you stand at the edge of a cliff,
blindfold tight and low across your eyes.

it cuts off your circulation,
presses into your flesh
until you hear the dull beating
of your own heart.
muted
drowning
the razor's edge.

the room is empty.
it was filled with hope, faith, trust and all the shit you're sold
through the narrow lense of society's
carnal desire to program you.

society is the true misanthrope.

you hear nothing but your own distant heartbeat,
which you can't reach anyway,
because that line is busy.

it's another life.
the promise.
the belief.
it's all a joke.

take the punch.
spit up blood.
feel the life in you.

don't look back.
no one cares anyway.

an open apology to Bukowski

I left *Love is a Dog from Hell* in room 609 of an over-styled,
yuppie hotel in Stockholm that would entice you to unleash
a torrent of rants about the vacuous nature of the guests
who stay there.

I did however pack my $72 bottle of Hermes perfume
I bought at duty free.

I know.

it should have been smokes and booze if I was a true acolyte.
but I felt ugly that day, so I went with the scent of platitudes
and phonies, instead of the elixir of truth.

the chocolate counter girl, who you'd fornicate with at the drop
of a quarter in a jukebox, asked me what perfume I was
wearing.

since she was French, I took it as a sign from the beauty gods that I,
indeed, had been transformed into a vessel of shimmering beauty.

still.

it doesn't make up for my weakness in substituting your nectars for vanity
and leaving your book of poems to sanitized Nordic white pagans in
Stockholm.

I take comfort in believing since the book was not found
in room 609, a salacious young immigrant in her
first housekeeping gig, waiting to be metaphorically set free,
rabidly tucked the book into her cafe latte B-cup and is secretly plotting
her next move with lust in her eyes between room 601 and 620.

sorry.
next time, I'll buy gin.

female misogynist

he's not a misogynist.

but his new 20-something, wanna-be feminist girlfriend is.

she worships Lena Dunham.
thinks Bukowski is a misogynist.

she hates sex.
so she fucks like a porn star.

she hates make-up.
but she wears mascara to fight off the label of lesbian.

she hates fashion.
but she wears faded, high-waisted ripped 80s jeans
because they're comfortable.

she hates him.

but she needs him to want her for all the things she isn't.
and all the things she thinks she should be.

all the things she can never be.

she's a cunt who controls him
with tiny lacerations of her tongue.

she's everything to him.
he's nothing to her.

loudmouth psyche

you are made of nothingness.

you have no atoms crashing into each other.

you aren't made of molecules and you have no cells.

you have no genomes so you can't be edited.

you can't reproduce or regenerate.

you scream at the top of your imaginary lungs
which hold no air.

I heard you once, but I put in those spongy, orange ear plugs
from Delta flight 45.

invaders

they always come in the back door.

omelets & white wine

they say Sunday is the Lord's day.

I think it's a cop-out on our behalf.

you gotta give a whole day away
to a guy you can't even see
smell or touch.

how did this happen?

what did the agenda look like in that meeting?
did the Lord even want this?

I think the Lord just wants a day to eat a nice fluffy buttery
omelette chased by a crisp, dry glass of Sancerre in a garden
and not have to think about how these fat white guys
ruined his day.

condensed milk

on the surface everything seems ok.

DH Lawrence hates mosquitos

it's not what he's known for.

but he really hates them.

he wrote a 450-word poem about hating just one mosquito.

one half inch, blood sucking winged creature that saws open your skin and uses six needles to suck your blood.

it only wants the protein in your blood to manufacture eggs.

so the mosquito needs you to procreate.

that's not so bad is it?

holy wafers & cheese whiz

I'm pretty sure the body of Christ
should taste better than a holy wafer.

holy wafers are an unholy marriage of a D+ science project
meets home economic class
under the bleachers on a Friday night.

salty yet bland.
gummy yet crisp.

it's a stupendously dysfunctional wafer.
it can't even sustain any pressure from a topping,
except cheese whiz.

it sticks to the roof of your mouth which reminds you of
Captain Crunch cereal which also sticks to the roof of your mouth,
but hurts more.

it doesn't even go with red wine.
a white would be better.

at least it's gluten free.

auto correct

why is the word fucking
ducking on your smartphone?

why does this pack of governmental circle jerks
decide what I can do?

what age I can smoke
what age I can drive
what age I can go forfeit my life for democracy

a permit to marry
a permit to drive
a permit to kill
a permit to keep a dog

a tax to pay on your
home
car
booze
snacks
smokes

why can't I type the word fucking to express my annoyance at
permits
laws
rules
taxes

and most importantly, auto-correct?

yellow mustard

you can't put yellow mustard on a ribeye in Texas.

love set apart by plate tectonics

apple of my eye
I gave my love a cherry
if you love something set it free
love is all you need
love isn't always on time
love me tender, love me dear.

for fucks sake, who believes this cataclysmic
train-wreck of verbal vomit?

the art of making letters into words
that turn into sentences that enslave us
to a way of thinking
that subdues our neocortex.

nihilism is more real than love.

algorithm

I know a guy who wakes up in the morning
and programs an algorithm that's
designed to create the most
torment
insult
hatred
loathing
fear

he isn't even aware it's running.

namiste

she found Jesus because he was free.
Depak Chopra costs big money.

he charges for the truth.

the Maharishi Mahesh yogi (or his followers)
will charge you $99.00 for the truth.

Jesus doesn't charge anything.

he just required her to be born again
and talk endlessly to the poor unsaved souls
who get sand in their shoes and have to sit on that one-legged
battered green park bench on Santa Monica beach dedicated
to Edith Klein to get the sand out.

she said she tried them all, but they cost too much.
the truth should be free.

she gestures to the sea
and asks if you know who made all of this.

she really doesn't want you to answer.
she just repeats her mantra needing to convince herself.
but it's too late.

Jesus already cashed that check and left the building.
because there's only one truth.

brown hair

his shoes are very big, his hair is very brown.
actually, it's perfectly brown.

it's the color brown of the brown crayon
in a crayola crayon box.

the kind of brown that only a color crayon company
would make.

the color crayon company had to understand brown.

they had to really know what brown meant
in order to turn it into the perfect brown
for the crayon box.

because brown isn't a color people get excited about.

it's just brown.
not purple
not green
not dark blue.

those colors have some life in them.
brown is just brown.
no one asks for brown anything.

yea, he had perfectly brown hair.

ghetto miracles

I believe in miracles.
I didn't say that, the band Hot Chocolate did in 1975.

I do believe in miracles.
only I don't believe.

believing means you're okay with standing in the middle of a
manic, gas-infused, four-lane highway
during the morning commute.

naked.

it means you don't mind sitting down on the yellow line
absorbing the heat from the dying star above you
sweating and choking from the fumes of your past.

believing leads to betrayal which only exists because you trust.

and believe.

Hot Chocolate said they believe in miracles,
but it was all about fucking for them.

in the end, that might just be the only miracle there is.

letters

in 1986 she wrote me one.

it was on lime green paper shaped like an apple.
maybe it was an apple green paper shaped like a lime.

It came all the way from Peaks Island, Maine to Cortona, Italy
with four tiny stamps and a disproportionately large air mail
sticker.

not a rubber stamp, but a sticker.

why would post office use a sticker and not a rubber stamp?

a rubber stamp says something.

it takes effort to stamp something. a stamp transfers the
emotions and passion of the person stamping your letter.

you can feel their mood in the shape of the stamp by the ink
that's left behind on your envelope.

a sticker is the suburban nightmare of conformity driven by
minivans and trips to costco.

she should have asked for the rubber air mail stamp.

artificial intelligence

we're on a loop.

we just don't believe it or know it.

we want to control our own destiny,
so we act horrible.

lie with pleasure
cheat with pride
steal with lust
hate with abandon
punch with love.

stagnate with purpose and justify with hedonism

carefully cut
measure
puncture
everything around us.

machines will inherit the earth you know.
from, on, with and by our loop.

truth

that's not my problem.

about the author

Love, Lust, Longing & Truth is the first book by
Southern writer and poet Jennifer Kite-Powell.
Kite-Powell adds honest angst, emotional logic
and candor to her work. Influenced by Charles
Bukowski, Bernadette Mayer and Harold Pinter
along with Mark Twain, Ranier Maria Rilke and
Milan Kundera, Kite-Powell brings a touch of
acerbic reality, mixed with longing and realistic
romanticism to her stream of consciousness
poems and short fiction. Her work in *Love,*
Lust, Longing & Truth evokes a feeling, a smell or emotion that leaves
you at the edge of comfort.

The author was born in San Antonio, Texas, grew up in Thomson, GA and has
spent the past decade floating free in Europe. She currently lives nowhere,
somewhere between here and there with her beagle Henry and writes about
science and technology for *Forbes*.

about the artist

Calato is a multi-disciplinary artist who is influ-
enced by her hometown Niagara Falls and it's
conflicted history of natural beauty and industrial
waste. Her art spans across installation, photogra-
phy and painting. The constant is always a desire
to create something that has lasting meaning
when it exits the walls of her studio. Calato lives
and works in New York City.

Made in the USA
San Bernardino, CA
16 February 2018